JESUS
Face to Face

MARK FINLEY with STEVEN MOSLEY

Pacific Press® Publishing Association
Nampa, Idaho
Oshawa, Ontario, Canada

Edited by Kenneth R. Wade
Cover designed by Judi Paliungas

Copyright © 1996 by
Pacific Press® Publishing Association
Printed in the United States of America

Finley, Mark, 1945-
   Jesus face to face / Mark Finley, with Steven Mosley.
      p.   cm.
   ISBN 0-8163-1374-1 (paper : alk. paper)
   1. Bible. N.T. Gospel—Biography. 2. Jesus
Christ—Friends and associates. 3. Christian life.
I. Mosley, Steven R., 1952-   . II. Title.
BS2430.F56   1996
232.9'5—dc21   96-46481
                                        CIP

98 99 00 • 5 4 3

Contents

Before You Turn This Page

The nation of Israel has dominated the news in recent months. The untimely assassination of Prime Minister Rabin, radical suicide bombings in Jerusalem in an attempt to interrupt the Middle East peace process, and the surprise election of a strongly conservative president has catapulted Israel into the forefront of the headlines. The world is focusing its attention on that sliver of land bordering the Mediterranean.

Recently our It Is Written production crew traveled to the land of Jesus to tape a new series of programs. The scripts for those programs are found here in our booklet, *Jesus Face to Face*. Personally, I'm convinced that there's only One who can bring peace to that troubled land. He's the One who brings Arab and Christian and Jew together. In Christ, barriers are broken down. In Christ, enemies become friends. In Christ, those separated for years are now reconciled and brought together. If Jesus' death can unite us as sinful human beings with God, He can certainly unite us with one another.

Steve and I would like to take you on a journey with us, a journey of discovery. As we travel back in time two thousand years and meet this Christ again in the pages of Scripture, we will sense with John that He washes away our anger. We will identify with the man by the Pool of Bethesda, that He saves us from the sidelines of life and thrusts us into a life of purpose and meaning. We, too, will sense, like Peter, that in Christ we find real courage. Like Mary who failed again and again, we will cry out, "He redeemed me from all my failures!" And like Nicodemus, we'll discover the meaning of true religion. Men and women met Him then, and they're meeting Him today. Peter and John, Mary and Nicodemus, the man by the Pool of Bethesda, each confronted Christ, each met Christ, and in Him they found love and acceptance, peace and mercy, and life-changing power.

As you read these pages, you may feel unusually lonely. You can find friendship in Jesus. You may feel unusually powerless and helpless and weak. You can find strength in Jesus. You may feel a burden of guilt crushing out your life. You can find forgiveness in Jesus, and that burden can be removed. You may feel confused, not knowing what choice to make regarding your future, and you can find direction in Jesus. You may feel lost, but in Jesus you are found. Christ meets our deepest human needs. Christ answers our inmost longings. In Him we find direction and purpose and meaning in our lives. As you read these pages, as you travel with us in your imagination to Israel, it's our prayer that you'll meet Him. It's our prayer that if you've met Him, you'll meet Him again and that your life will be forever different because you've journeyed with us through these pages to meet Him.

He Washed Away
My Anger

Have you noticed lately how many people are getting angry in the name of God, fighting mad in the name of religion? It happens even in the holy city of Jerusalem, a place considered sacred by Christians, Jews and Muslims.

What lies behind all these loud, raging voices? Is it righteous indignation? Or something more sinister?

This is the remarkable story of a very angry young man who discovered a very different kind of religion.

John was asked to make arrangements for lodging in the town up ahead, and he seemed glad to be of service. He was the youngest of the twelve men Jesus had chosen to be His apostles. But already he'd shown leadership qualities.

John, accompanied by his brother James, hurried on down a rocky hill toward the village in the fading light, determined to make the Master proud of him. True, making arrangements might be a bit tricky. After all, this was Samaria, a place most Jews avoided. There had been bad blood between Jews and Samaritans since long before John was born.

In fact, most people traveling from Galilee down to Jerusalem, as Jesus was, avoided the land of Samaria altogether. They took a detour through Perea.

But Jesus had chosen the direct route south. And as John hurried his steps along the dusty road, he was reminded of another occasion when his Master had done the same thing.

Jesus had once stopped in Samaria, stopped at a well just outside the town of Sychar. And He'd asked a woman at the well there for a drink of water. They began a conversation. The woman rushed off to tell her friends about this remarkable Man. And in the end, many of the residents of Sychar came to believe in Jesus as the Messiah.

That encounter stuck in John's mind. Later, he would write about it in detail. And now, as he walked through the town gate, John thought something similar might happen with this visit.

John and James asked around for lodging. A great teacher named Jesus would be spending the night, they said. Middle Eastern custom dictated that hospitality always be shown to strangers. At first, the Samaritans tried to oblige. But then they heard that Jesus was actually on His way to Jerusalem to celebrate a great feast at the temple.

The Samaritans folded their arms and pressed their lips together. No, they could not shelter a party intending to honor their religious rivals in Jerusalem.

John tried to reason with them. Did they know who this Jesus was? Hadn't they heard of the great wonders He'd performed?

The Samaritans wouldn't budge.

So, John and James had to leave town and head back up the hill to meet Jesus. And as John walked, he grew more and more angry. He kept seeing those stubborn Samaritan faces, shaking their heads.

John wasn't used to being insulted. He'd grown up in a very comfortable home in Bethsaida. His father operated a prosperous fishing business—with hired servants. His mother was a woman of some means. The family had connections with the high priest in Jerusalem.

Who did these poor Samaritans think they were?

And what really galled John was that they'd refused shelter to his Master. Just days before this, John had stood on a mountaintop with Jesus and watched in awe. Christ became a dazzling, divine figure right before his eyes. And Moses and Elijah appeared from heaven to honor Christ.

John had seen his Master shining like the sun. And now these Samaritans presumed their wretched village was too good for Him. Incredible.

By the time John met up with Jesus, his indignation was about to explode. John and his brother quickly explained the situation. And then, perhaps John's eye turned to Mount Carmel in the distance, the place where Elijah had called down fire from heaven, the place where the prophets of Baal had been struck down.

Filled with zeal, John burst out with these words, recorded in Luke 9. " 'Lord, do You want us to command fire to come down from heaven and consume them, just as Elijah did?' " (Luke 9:54, NKJV).

John wanted to demonstrate His loyalty. He wanted those who'd dishonored his Christ to be crushed.

But Jesus looked away from him. He gazed down for a moment at the cluster of houses barely visible in the dusk. Then He turned back to John and said: " 'You do not know what manner of spirit you are of. For the Son of Man did not come to destroy men's lives but to save them' " (Luke 9:55, 56, NKJV).

And then Jesus suggested they try at the next village.

John's Master understood him much better than he understood himself. When He called John and James to be among the Twelve, He gave them a nickname. He called them "Sons of Thunder."

These young men had plenty of fire in the belly. They

were gung-ho, ready to go. And Jesus saw their potential. But He also understood, much more clearly than they, that the fire could burn in two very different directions. And standing there, looking down on that Samaritan village, Jesus pointed out the two directions. He did not come to destroy men's lives, but to save them.

In this book, *Jesus Face to Face*, we're going to be looking at the impact of Christ's face-to-face encounters with five very interesting individuals. And we're going to see how skillfully Christ met specific, felt needs through these encounters. We're going to get a dramatic picture of just how Jesus can meet our own deepest needs.

Now, back to John's story. You know, zeal for the truth, passion for a just cause, can drive us to destroy those we receive as enemies, or it can drive us to redeem them.

John hadn't been able to see that distinction. He didn't know what kind of spirit was driving him. He thought it was a spirit of loyalty and fervor. He didn't see the raw anger inside, the destructive anger.

John was a very earnest, sincere young man. John was also a very angry young man. That's the challenge Jesus took on in one of His disciples.

It's a challenge that many people must deal with in their own lives. A great deal of what passes for righteous indignation these days conceals a great deal of anger. People use religious battles with enemies to cover up personal battles with anger.

Secular people do the same thing in different ways. We see people spend their whole lives fighting *against* something. Maybe it's against pollution or the abuse of animals. Their cause is fine. But their attitude is dominated by rage and anger.

Employers and supervisors fall into this as well. They may think it's necessary to be aggressive; they may think they have to keep pushing people to get anything done.

But it's really anger that's driving them on. It's anger that keeps them pushing. They have to get it out in some way.

Again, being zealous is not the problem. Having zeal for a cause is not the problem. It's living our lives based on anger that's destructive. Religion based on anger is destructive. Careers based on anger are destructive.

Bad things happen to all of us in this life. Bad things can happen to us in childhood. Bad things can happen to us as we go through school. Friends can betray us. Spouses can abuse us.

And sometimes those bad things seep down deep inside. We can't forget. We can't forgive. The wound doesn't heal. And anger starts building up. We want so badly to change that bad thing that happened to us. We want to fix it. We want to get even.

But we can't change the past. So our anger keeps seeping out in all kinds of ways. We find ourselves raging against some group as the enemy—because deep inside we're raging against something our parents did. We find ourselves calling fire down from heaven on some town, because deep inside we're still wounded.

What can we do about this kind of anger? What can replace it? How do we keep indignation from becoming a cloak for rage?

Well, let's take a look at how Christ dealt with His angry young man. Because something remarkable happened to John, the Son of Thunder.

We move many months past that run-in between John and the inhospitable Samaritan village. The scene: an upper room somewhere in Jerusalem. It had been reserved for the Passover meal Christ wanted to celebrate with His twelve disciples.

And as they gathered in the lengthening shadows of evening, these men could sense that something significant was going to happen. Walking up the stairs to the upper room, they started talking about the kingdom Christ had promised to establish.

And then their eyes fell on the low table where the Passover meal had been laid out. They looked down at the pillows arranged around three sides of the table where they would be reclining.

This was a formal Passover supper. Who would be sitting where? Who would have the honored positions next to Christ?

Well, as human nature would have it, all twelve felt highly qualified. All had absorbed Christ's teachings. All had performed miracles in His name. All had proclaimed the Good News in His Name. John wasn't the only highly driven individual in this crowd.

And standing there awkwardly, these men found themselves bickering about where to sit. They just couldn't help it. The twelve had spent a long time together, plenty of time to acquire grudges and resentments.

In the end, Judas managed to maneuver his way to one side of Christ. After all, as he always reminded the rest, he was the treasurer. And John reclined on the other side. The others slowly stretched out around the table and looked daggers at Judas and John.

It was time to celebrate the Passover, the memorial of God's great deliverance of Israel from Egypt. But the air in the upper room seemed heavy that evening. It seemed that all the resentful words the disciples had muttered were still suspended there.

Suddenly, Christ rose to His feet. He stepped over to a water basin. At first, the disciples assumed it was time for the ritual hand-washing that was part of the Passover meal.

But then, Jesus laid aside His outer garment. He took a towel and tucked it into His waistband. He poured water from a pitcher into the basin and then moved back toward His disciples.

Kneeling down, He removed one man's sandals. And without a word, He began to bathe the man's feet. He washed the dirt and grime of the streets of Jerusalem from his toes.

And then, Jesus moved to the next man.

John watched this in awe. There was Jesus, the picture of a slave performing his menial task. But it wasn't something menial, this washing of feet. It wasn't just a dirty chore. To John, it seemed something quite glorious.

He stared at Jesus' hands as the Master worked, washing, drying, from one disciple to the next. Those were remarkable hands. He'd seen them work before.

He'd seen them take a little girl's pale, lifeless hand as the family wept and wailed around her. He'd watched as Christ's hands lifted the child from her deathbed.

John had seen those hands touch a paralytic staring helplessly at the Pool of Bethesda. He'd seen the man rise and walk.

John had seen those hands lifted in prayer before a hungry crowd of five thousand. He'd seen those hands break a few loaves of bread into a meal that satisfied them all.

He'd seen those hands lifted to defend a woman caught in the act of adultery from those ready to stone her.

John had seen those hands touch the eyes of a man born blind—and create sight where none existed before.

He'd seen those hands beckon to His friend, Lazarus, who'd been in a tomb for four days. And Lazarus responded.

John had seen those hands do a lot during his time with Jesus. And it all came over him as he stared at Jesus washing the soiled feet of His disciples. Those were powerful hands. They were omnipotent hands. But above all, they were the hands of love.

They blessed whatever they touched. They had come to save, not to destroy.

At length, Jesus came to John and undid his sandals. He began to wash his feet. And at that moment, it didn't seem to matter who was sitting where at the table. It didn't matter who would be most honored in the kingdom. This incredible love was all that mattered.

And as Jesus washed John's feet, the Son of Thunder felt his anger being washed away at last. Christ's love had finally overcome it. Christ's love was stronger than all the hurt, all the rage, all the misguided zeal.

Years later, John would remember this crucial moment in his life. He would remember how much it meant to him.

This is the way he would describe it. "Jesus, knowing that the Father had given all things into His hands, and that He had come from God and was going to God, rose from supper and laid aside His garments, took a towel and girded himself. After that, He poured water into a basin and began to wash the disciples' feet" (John 13:3-5, NKJV).

Jesus had performed the slave's menial chore *knowing* that He had come from God and was going to God. Jesus deserved to be exalted to the highest place in heaven. But He had occupied the lowest on earth.

John was overwhelmed by the Master's gracious act. At last, he'd found something to replace his religion of anger. It was love, pure and simple. All of Jesus' life came together in that one beautiful act in the upper room.

As a Christian, when I participate in the foot-washing service in my church, I feel that love flowing through my heart again.

Friends, Jesus has a solution for people consumed by anger. He has a solution for those whose religion is driven by anger, for those whose restless drive in life is motivated by anger.

You can never do enough to quench that anger. You can never accomplish enough to get even with the bad things that happened. There's always more anger left over at the end.

It's only love that can quench our anger. It's only love that can heal the wounds. We can never, never change the past. But we *can* be loved in the present.

And here's how it happens. John was transformed in the end because he had experienced three-and-a-half years of fellowship with Jesus. We can fellowship with Him in His Word. I've found certain passages of Scripture very helpful in dealing with my own anger. Reading the epistles of John and meditating on the beautiful Christian love he emphasizes—that has helped to break anger in my own heart.

Jesus is capable of pouring His love into our hearts. Here's how. Jesus wants us to open ourselves up to Him— so He can wash our feet, so He can show us what gracious love is all about. Jesus can wash away our anger.

He did it for John. He transformed the fiery Son of Thunder. Toward the end of John's life we find him in chains on the Isle of Patmos, imprisoned for his faith. He knows that he will probably die alone—separated from the believers who mean everything to him.

But John doesn't rage on that island. He doesn't call down fire from heaven on the Roman soldiers who guard him. He doesn't anguish because he won't occupy an honored position in the kingdom at the end of his earthly life.

No, instead John writes. He sends out epistles. And they are some of the most beautiful love letters this world has ever seen. Oh, John was still thundering at the end. He still had fire in his belly. He still had plenty of passion and zeal. But now it was love that he thundered out. It was love that compelled him. John had become the Apostle of Love.

"My little children," John writes to believers in the epistle we know as First John. He calls them his "beloved." And over and over he urges, "love one another," "love in deed and truth," "There is no fear in love," "We love, because He first loved us."

Have you experienced the kind of gracious love that transformed this Son of Thunder? Or are you still driven by anger? We can try to replace our pain and rage in countless ways. But there's only one real solution. Only love can wash away our anger.

He Redeemed
All My Failures

She was one of the faithful few, one who remained at the scene of the cross when Jesus died at the site called the Place of the Skull.

She was the first human being to see Him after His resurrection.

Still, we seem to know so little about Mary—this other Mary.

But we'll find out about the secret that transformed her life.

The disciples of Christ had almost all been scared away the night before. It seemed that only His enemies, and the stone-faced Roman soldiers, were left at the scene now. It was, after all, a crucifixion, a spectacle designed to terrorize, to put fear into the heart of anyone who might challenge the authorities.

The condemned man had been suspended on two beams. It would take hours for Him to die. Few people could stomach watching this agony up close. The only voices you could hear at this Place of the Skull were those of priests and scribes mocking the One they had worked so hard to have executed.

But a few brave, friendly faces remained. A group of women maintained a silent vigil as the soldiers carried out their gruesome work. And the one named first among them was—Mary Magdalene, Mary from the town of Magdala.

She stood by on that Friday afternoon as Jesus made His blood-curdling cry, "My God, My God, why have you forsaken me?"

She stood by as the soldiers gambled over His tunic.

She stood by when the sun was blotted out and when the earth shook.

Mary kept her vigil until the very end, until Jesus said, "It is finished," drew a last raspy breath, shuddered, and slumped against the spikes. She couldn't turn away—even when a soldier ran his spear into Jesus' side to make sure He was dead.

We know that Mary Magdalene kept her vigil because she was still there when Jesus' broken body was taken down from the cross. She, and a few other women companions, followed Joseph of Arimathea when he carried the body to his garden tomb.

As the shadows lengthened late on Friday afternoon, she saw exactly where her Master was laid to rest. And then she hurried home to prepare spices and perfumes to complete His burial.

Mary's vigil shows us a remarkable devotion, a remarkable loyalty. It's a vigil that stands in contrast to the behavior of Christ's disciples. During those darkest hours—where were the men who had followed Jesus for three years? The brightest and strongest and most zealous weren't there. Where was Peter—who'd vowed to die for his Lord? Where was the resourceful Matthew? Where were Philip and Andrew?

Their Master had suddenly been caught up in a tragedy. And that tragedy had overwhelmed them. Their faith had fallen apart.

But Mary Magdalene remained devoted. She remained

at the scene. She stood steadfast when strong men ran away.

Why? What was the secret of this woman's strength and devotion? What lay behind her heroic vigil?

I want to suggest an answer, an answer that we glimpse in one of her encounters with Christ. It's an answer that is reinforced by something similar that happened to other individuals like her in the Gospels.

Now, let's see what happened to Mary Magdalene. The first encounter between Mary and Christ is not described in detail. We don't have a complete story of what occurred. But we do have this statement. Luke tells us what happened early on in the ministry of Christ: "Jesus traveled about from one town and village to another, proclaiming the good news of the kingdom of God. The Twelve were with him, and also some women who had been cured of evil spirits and diseases: Mary (called Magdalene) from whom seven demons had come out" (Luke 8:1, 2, NIV).

The first one Luke mentions among the women who ministered to Jesus in His travels is Mary Magdalene. Mark identifies her in the same way that Luke does: "Mary Magdalene, out of whom [Jesus] had driven seven demons" (Mark 16:9, NIV).

Let's think about this a moment. Not many people get down to the point where they are actually possessed by a demon, the point where some compulsion just takes over their lives. But Mary had somehow reached that point. Some evil thing had control of her.

The Bible doesn't tell us what the problem was. It seems that her home town of Magdala had a bad reputation. Its citizens had grown prosperous in the manufacture and dying of fine woolen fabrics. There was plenty of money floating around—and with it plenty of vice. Rabbis would later attribute the destruction of Magdala to its moral corruption.

Mary had grown up in this environment—and ultimately, through continued sin, she became demon possessed. But that's not all. The Gospel writers tell us that Jesus had to drive out *seven* demons from this woman.

That's a lot of problems for one person to have, a lot of compulsions, a lot of being out of control. We don't know whether Jesus drove all the demons out at once or whether Mary had to come back seven times for repeated healing. In any case, her life must have been a mess, a tragic mess.

Now, it may be hard for many of you to relate to someone possessed by seven demons. But I'm sure you *do* know of people who seem to have been born with more than their share of problems. Their background, their childhood, conspires against them. It's left them bitter or terribly insecure. And life seems to go downhill from there.

Take a young woman I'll call Jan, for example. Jan was brought up in a Christian home, but she rebelled against the values of her parents. She felt they were manipulative and controlling.

So Jan set out to explore the world on her own. By the time she was fifteen, she had slipped into alcohol and drug abuse. These became addictions that she could never quite shake.

Jan tried to find the love she needed, with a succession of men. She lived with several boyfriends but could never settle down, never experienced a really stable relationship.

Sometimes Jan would visit the church of her childhood. I remember her at some evangelistic meetings I conducted. Jan was interested, but she could never quite grasp the real power and presence of God. Several times she came forward after an appeal; several times she determined to stop abusing drugs. But each time, she went back to the old life. The pull was just too strong.

It was terribly frustrating to try to help Jan. You wanted

her to experience God's love; you wanted her to grasp what a relationship with Him could mean. But it kept slipping through her fingers. It remained painfully out of reach.

Life just kept spiraling downward for Jan. It all started with typical adolescent rebellion. But one problem led to another. The problems kept getting bigger. And pretty soon Jan's life was out of control.

We have a word for people like Jan. It's not a very kind word. We dismiss them as "losers." They're messed up. They've got all kinds of problems. They'll never get their act together.

Friends, Mary Magdalene was a loser, a seven-time loser. One problem had led to another. The problems kept getting bigger, until finally she became demon possessed.

But this woman, this failure, experienced a profound kind of deliverance through her encounter with Christ. Something happened to her that turned her into that steadfast woman keeping her heroic vigil at the cross.

And may I suggest it was more than just an exorcism. Because, as Jesus Himself pointed out, you have to put something better *in* when you drive something demonic *out*. Losers don't get a life just because they're no longer demon possessed.

I believe we start to see the answer in something Jesus said about seven-time losers. Once Peter came up to Him and asked how many times he was obligated to forgive someone who continued to mess up. Peter thought he was being generous when he said, "Up to seven times?"

Jesus replied with these words in Matthew: . . . " 'I do not say to you, up to seven times, but up to seventy times seven' " (Matthew 18:22, NKJV).

In other words, just keep on forgiving. Jesus didn't want to put any limits on forgiveness. And it was more than just quantity—pardoning someone over and over again. The *quality* of Jesus' forgiveness was also limitless.

When Mary came to Jesus with her repeated failures, He didn't just wave off the offense like a judge reluctantly giving a seven-time loser one more chance. Jesus accepted her graciously. He forgave generously. He was willing to wrestle with the demons on her behalf.

I believe it was the *quality* of Christ's forgiveness that transformed this woman so profoundly. That was the key element in her encounter with Christ.

The Bible itself suggests that. Let's look at a certain scene Luke tells about in his Gospel. "The women who followed him from Galilee, stood at a distance, watching these things" (Luke 23:49, NKJV).

Mary Magdalene kept her vigil with a group of other women, women who kept their devotion alive in the darkest hour. Think of some of the women Christ encountered during His ministry. Think of some of the failures He encountered.

There was the woman who was caught by the Pharisees in the act of adultery. Now please remember, in Jesus' time, this wasn't something that got you on talk shows. This was something that got you stoned to death.

But Jesus disarmed her accusers with one deft stroke. He declared: . . . " 'He who is without sin among you, let him throw a stone at her first' " (John 8:7, NKJV).

And the vengeful men melted away.

I think it's significant that when Jesus asked her, "Has no one condemned you?" she answered meekly, "No one, Lord."

This woman called Jesus "Lord." He had quietly removed her tormentors from the scene. When she looked up, they were gone. It's no wonder she called Him Lord.

Jesus showed such a gracious way, almost an understated way, of expressing forgiveness: "If all those angry, indignant people aren't condemning you anymore, well, I certainly won't either."

At the worst moment in her life, this woman heard those gentle words of encouragement. Of course, she called Him Lord.

We see the quality of Christ's forgiveness even more clearly in another encounter He had with a failure.

One evening, Jesus went to dine at the home of a Pharisee named Simon. It was rather early in Jesus' ministry. He was just beginning to attract attention. Some thought He might even be a prophet. So, of course, the best people in town were there to check Him out.

But one person managed to slip in uninvited—through the open courtyard, mingling for a bit with the servants, then up the veranda steps and into the festive dining hall. No one noticed her at first; the room was crowded with people conversing.

But then, they began to smell something pungent, something very different from the aroma of the food on the table. It smelled like perfume.

As the guests paused to take this in, they heard the sound of a woman sobbing. And then, Simon spotted her, bent over Jesus' feet as He reclined at the table. Here was his guest of honor, accosted by a stranger. The woman's tears fell on Jesus' feet, and she was wiping them with her hair and pouring expensive perfume on them from an alabaster vial.

Simon was unnerved by this rude interruption. But he really got upset when he got a glimpse of her face. This woman was known all over town for her immorality.

How could it be then, that this Jesus was allowing her to touch Him? *If He really was a prophet*, Simon thought, *then surely He would know what kind of a person she was.*

In the middle of all this disturbance, Jesus proceeded to tell Simon a story. A certain moneylender had two debtors. One owed 500 dollars, the other 50. Both were unable to pay and so the moneylender just canceled both their debts. "Which of them," Jesus asked, "will love him more?"

Simon had listened patiently, and he answered, "I suppose the one who was forgiven more."

But he couldn't see what this had to do with that woman making a spectacle of herself.

So Jesus told him plainly. When I came in, you didn't wash my feet. But this woman has bathed them with her tears. You didn't anoint my head, but she has anointed my feet with perfume.

And then He uttered these words: " 'Therefore . . . her sins, which are many, are forgiven, for she loved much. But to whom little is forgiven, the same loves little' " (Luke 7:47, NKJV).

Then Jesus turned to the woman and whispered, "Your sins are forgiven."

Everyone in that room had expected this woman, whom they regarded as a social outcast, to be put in her place.

Well, Jesus did. He put her at the head of the table. He explained that only she truly understood what it means to be forgiven. And she had responded with a wealth of devotion. Jesus made this notorious failure an example for them all.

He who is forgiven much, loves much.

That's the secret behind those women keeping their vigil at the cross. Jesus had many other followers at the time. Many others intended to be loyal. Many others wanted to believe in Him. But they weren't there. Almost all the disciples had fled the scene.

But he who is forgiven much, loves much. That's what those women had—an appreciation for the quality of Christ's forgiveness. And it inspired a devotion that no dark night, no terrible execution, could blot out.

Have you ever felt like a failure? Maybe you're not a seven-time loser like Mary Magdalene or Jan. But maybe you've struggled with a habit that trips you up, over and over again. Maybe you've felt imprisoned by the same destructive emotions, over and over again. Maybe you know what it's like to try to come to God in repentance for the same old thing, when you've already come countless times before.

You feel like such a hypocrite. You feel like a loser.

Well, I want you to take heart from that extraordinary group of people keeping their vigil at the cross. I want you to know that Jesus' forgiveness is like nothing else; Jesus' forgiveness can ennoble.

He who is forgiven much, can love much.

How? We have to grasp the worth of the Forgiver. We have to receive forgiveness in the same whole-hearted way as that woman wiping Jesus' feet with her hair.

Your failures can be redeemed by Christ's forgiveness—*if* you really come to appreciate what that act means, if you sense how graciously Christ forgives, if you touch the heart of the forgiver. If you understand the worth of the One who extends forgiveness.

That's how we are changed. A lot of human forgiveness is really a condescending put-down. But Jesus' forgiveness lifts us up. It lifted Mary Magdalene up. It made her the first to bear witness to the most glorious event in human history.

Early on Sunday morning, Mary came to the tomb of Christ with her spices and ointments to care for His body. But to her astonishment, the stone had been rolled away from the tomb's entrance, and the body had disappeared.

Mary hurried back into Jerusalem to tell Peter and John. Someone had taken Christ's body. We don't know where they've laid Him. She still couldn't grasp the idea of a resurrection.

The two disciples ran to the Garden Tomb and saw the grave clothes lying inside—but no body. Peter and John went back to tell the others the strange news.

But Mary couldn't leave the scene. She couldn't bear the thought of never being able to honor her Master at His grave. She just stood there weeping for some time. Mary was keeping another vigil.

And then she heard a voice ask, "Woman, why are you crying? Who are you looking for?"

Mary looked up and at first didn't quite recognize the man through her tears. She assumed he was the caretaker and asked about Christ's body.

You can hear the pleading, the longing in her voice, when she asks: . . . " 'Sir, if You have carried Him away, tell me where You have laid Him, and I will take Him away' " (John 20:15, NKJV).

Then the man called her by name, "Mary!" And that voice went right through her. It was the same loving voice that had given her hope as a seven-time loser. The same strong voice that had cast out her demons.

Mary looked up and exclaimed "Rabboni, Teacher!" She rushed to where Christ stood, threw herself down at His feet. This was too wonderful to be true. She'd watched as crucifixion drained the life out of this Man. And there He stood, healthy and radiant. It was overwhelming. Yes, as overwhelming as Christ's forgiveness.

And there by that garden tomb, clutching Jesus' feet, Mary Magdalene was the woman who loved much. She was the woman caught in adultery, saved from humiliation. She was the woman anointing Jesus' feet with her tears. She was all of them. She was all those who'd failed terribly. All those who'd been terribly shamed.

And above all, she was one who was ennobled by forgiveness. She was one whom forgiveness had made heroic.

Christ gave her the most important of commissions. . . . " 'Go to My brethren and say to them, "I am ascending to My Father and your Father, and to My God and your

God" ' " (John 20:17, NKJV).

And so, Mary Magdalene became the first and foremost witness of Christ's resurrection. She was the first to say, "I have seen Him alive from the dead." She could testify that He was on His way to the Father, to seal in the courts of heaven, the forgiveness He had bestowed on earth.

She who is forgiven much, loves much.

Have you discovered the *quality* of Christ's forgiveness? Have you grasped the worth of the One who extends this grace? Your failures, your humiliations, can become a tool in God's hands. They can help you finally know from the heart, the height and depth and breadth and length of Christ's forgiveness.

He Lightened My Pride

He was an intellectual who studied at the temple in Jerusalem. His life centered around that holy site.

But one time he went outside—asking questions. However, he wanted to make sure they were answered—at night.

And what he never dreamed was that the answers wouldn't come until what seemed to be one of the darkest days in history.

The light would finally dawn on him as he tenderly handled a corpse.

A spring wind was sweeping through the narrow streets of Jerusalem. Night had settled over the city, and most of its citizens were in their homes, preparing for bed. But one dignified, prominent religious leader walked in the dark with a determined look on his face. His destination was a certain spot on the slopes of the Mount of Olives, the place where Jesus of Nazareth often retired to pray.

He had been going through quite a struggle to get to this point. This man was a member of the Sanhedrin, the supreme Jewish court of justice. His name, Nicodemus, meant "victor over the people." He occupied a very important position in society. And everything in his aristocratic

29

background, everything in the beliefs held by his peers, told him not to make this visit.

This Jesus, after all, had attacked their center of power—the sacred temple in Jerusalem. He had boldly driven out the merchants, who provided animals for the sacrifices, as if the temple were His private domain.

Everyone around Nicodemus had come to regard Jesus as an enemy. But Nicodemus had always prided himself on being a fair-minded man, a rational man. So he did a little investigating. He listened. He listened to the people who were claiming Jesus had performed miracles. It was hard to deny that something remarkable was happening. The more he heard, the more Nicodemus felt convicted that, fundamentally, Jesus was a good man.

But this posed a terrible dilemma. Nicodemus, as a Pharisee, had always believed that he stood for integrity, for the law of God. But Jesus seemed to be in constant conflict with the Pharisees. If He was a good man, how could this be?

Finally, Nicodemus decided he *had* to check Jesus out for himself. But he would go at night. He told himself that if he went openly, others might follow his example. And he wasn't at all yet sure about this Galilean rabbi.

What Nicodemus couldn't admit to himself was that he feared what his peers might say. It was a bit humiliating to be seen chasing after this crowd-pleasing miracle worker.

Nicodemus came up to the olive grove where Jesus was meditating. Coming face to face with Jesus, Nicodemus said: " 'Rabbi, we know that You are a teacher come from God; for no one can do these signs that You do unless God is with him' " (John 3:2, NKJV).

Now, when Nicodemus said "we," he was referring to the Pharisees. But in fact, this "we" didn't know any such thing. Most Pharisees regarded Jesus more as a son of Beelzebub than a "teacher come from God."

So, Nicodemus was, in part, just trying to be polite. Also, he thought he might get Jesus to open up if he spoke of His ministry in the best terms.

Well, Jesus did open up—in ways Nicodemus hadn't bargained for. Without pausing, without any little chit-chat, Jesus frankly made this famous reply: " 'Most assuredly, I say to you, unless one is born again, he cannot see the kingdom of God' " (John 3:3, NKJV).

Nicodemus didn't know what to say. He'd apparently just been diagnosed, and prescribed some drastic medicine. But what was the disease? Nicodemus himself hadn't hinted that he was ill.

Nicodemus, the scholar, had to think fast if he was going to keep this interview on the level of a pleasant discussion. So he asked, in disbelief: " 'How can a man be born when he is old? Can he enter a second time into his mother's womb and be born?' " (John 3:4, NKJV).

Nicodemus knew better than to take Jesus' words this literally. The Jewish priests themselves sometimes spoke of Gentile converts as children just born. And they used the same metaphor to describe a bridegroom at his marriage and a king at his enthronement.

So Nicodemus was doing a little intellectual fencing with this Jesus, this adversary of the Pharisees.

But Jesus simply pressed His point home. He said He was talking about a spiritual re-birth, not something physical. He described the Spirit as an invisible force that moves through human life—like the wind moving over a landscape.

Nicodemus was growing quite uncomfortable now. After all, he was at the very top of Jewish society, at the very top of religious society. He was accustomed to issuing verdicts and handing out judgments, *not* receiving pointed advice. But here, this Galilean teacher was telling him he had to be born again—spiritually; he had to start all over again. That was a bit much to take.

Nicodemus found himself trying to fend off Jesus' remarks. He was more convicted than perplexed. But he asked skeptically, "How can these things be?"

Jesus refused to detour into a debate. He very earnestly told this Pharisee that He was showing him the way to eternal life, that God loved the world so much He gave up His Son, that whoever believes in Him is not condemned, and that human beings are judged by how they respond to the light given them.

By the time Nicodemus made his way back down the slope of the Mount of Olives toward Jerusalem, he'd heard quite an earful. The interview hadn't gone at all like he'd expected. He'd come to check out Jesus. But he himself had been held up to the light. And his first instinct was to run from it as fast as he could.

Nicodemus faced a question that we all must face: What does it mean to be born again? What Jesus was trying to point out was the radical nature of the new birth. The Spirit of God coming into a person's life, Jesus said, is like a wind blowing over a landscape; it may be an invisible force, but it affects everything in its path.

To be born again means to start all over—as a spiritual creature. Individuals stuck in time get in touch with eternity. Individuals mired in the problems of the world are transformed by the values of heaven.

Let me give you another analogy. In one sense being born again is like learning a new language. Let's say you visit Mexico—but can't speak a word of Spanish. That country, that culture, is pretty much closed up to you. But if you study the language and practice it and master it—then it's like a whole new world opening up. You understand all that's going on around you.

The challenge of being born again is the challenge of living in a whole new world, a spiritual world where Jesus Christ reigns.

Nicodemus would have to face a choice, an all-important choice. It was a choice between remaining a questioning skeptic, and becoming a devoted follower, a choice between remaining where he was, and entering that new world.

To better understand his predicament, let's take a look at a few other skeptics in the New Testament. When the Pharisees and Sadducees decided that Jesus posed a terrible threat, they began to try to discredit him.

They sent out bright young men, lawyers and scribes who posed as truth seekers, to ask Jesus questions—questions designed to entrap. Like hostile news reporters today, these men tried to catch Jesus saying something that could get Him in trouble with the authorities, or at least something that sounded stupid.

The Jewish leaders were watching Jesus' every move. They had their spies everywhere. They believed they could expose Jesus as an imposter. Nicodemus was a part of this world. He was probably more earnest and honest than many of his peers. But he was a member of the "opposition."

And the opposition was always ready with questions:

"Is it lawful to pay taxes to Caesar?"

"If a woman has seven husbands who all die one after the other, whose wife will she be in the resurrection?"

It was all a game, a very serious and deadly game, but a game. The questions weren't about getting answers, they were about setting one up, about trapping the opponent, about proving who was right.

No one was looking for the good word that might change their hearts. They were looking for words they could bounce around in their heads.

A lawyer came up one day and asked Jesus, "Which is the greatest commandment in the law?"

Yes, lawyers could occupy themselves endlessly on that one. They could carry on very abstract arguments about which principle had priority over another.

Jesus, however, summed it up very neatly with a statement from the book of Deuteronomy: " 'You shall love the Lord your God with all your heart, with all your soul, and with all your might' " (Deuteronomy 6:5, NKJV).

Everything hangs on that.

But the spies were not after clarity. Scoring points was the goal. Winning the debate was the thing.

Jesus wanted people to face the truth about themselves. The spies wanted to hide behind the truth.

Do you realize that you can do that? Yes, you can hide behind the truth. You can use it as a shield, hold it out there in front of you, wield it as a weapon, win arguments with it, score points with it. You can hide behind the truth.

You can quote it so well that nobody notices you're not dealing with the real problems inside. You can show off the correct state of your mind so that no one notices the painful state of your heart.

Friends, you can hide behind the truth. It's not enough for you to have the right answers. It's not enough for you to be able to quote God's principles. If it's not touching your heart, it's not the truth; it's something else. If you're not allowing God to apply it in your own life, then it's not the truth, it's something else.

This is the dilemma that Nicodemus faced. The part of him that was a skeptic wanted to hide behind the truth. But another part of him wanted to take Jesus' words to heart. The proud Pharisee wanted to justify himself. The honest seeker wanted to be taught.

It was a real struggle there on the Mount of Olives. And unfortunately pride almost won out. Nicodemus asked questions only to fend off conviction. He'd spent most of his life intellectualizing everything. And old habits are hard to change.

But something very important had happened anyway. Nicodemus had heard Jesus' words—face to face. And he couldn't make those words go away. They kept trying to get down into his heart, despite all the mental games he could play.

The skeptic was slowly turning into a follower, or at least he was taking definite steps in that direction. We catch a glimpse of this in a certain meeting of the Sanhedrin.

They were grilling some officers who had been sent out to bring in Jesus for questioning. The officers had failed to do this. And the only explanation they could offer was: "No man ever spoke like this Man!"

The Sanhedrin rulers were, of course, very upset saying, in effect: "It's only the ignorant crowd that follows this Galilean Jesus. None of us believe in Him."

And it was at this point that Nicodemus stood up among his peers and said these words, recorded in John 7: " 'Does our law judge a man before it hears him and knows what he is doing?' " (John 7:51, NKJV).

It was only a question. It may have been only a timid attempt to turn back the tide of prejudice. But Nicodemus had taken a step. He had exposed himself to the scorn of his peers, the elite of Jerusalem.

They immediately shot back at him: "Prophets just don't come out of Galilee. Are you also from Galilee?" It was a way of saying, "Are you also a country bumpkin?"

Nicodemus had to do some hard thinking after this. Because it became more and more evident that his friends in the Sanhedrin were acting out of jealousy and hatred.

They could make their opposition to Jesus sound very pious. But the murderous tone in their voices was unmistakable.

And yet, how could he turn his back on the Sanhedrin? It seemed like turning his back on the Law of God itself. And he would lose everything. He had made it to the top. How could he risk everything?

Well, the moment of truth came for Nicodemus at a most unexpected time. It came at a very dark, frightening time. And it came at the scene of a horrible crime.

Jesus the Galilean was dying on a Roman cross. The blood was draining from his head and wrists and feet at Golgotha. And the friends of Nicodemus were circling that cross, mocking their defeated enemy. They suggested that if He was really such a miracle worker, He should come down from the cross and save Himself.

The best and the brightest of the Sanhedrin were staring at what they thought was their final argument: no man blessed of God would be given over to such a terrible fate. They had been proven right. They'd been right all along about Jesus.

When a Roman soldier finally plunged his spear into Jesus' side and blood gushed out, when the body hung pale and limp, they gloated over their victory. All the scribes and rulers and priests could look on—and feel themselves proved right. All the spies could look on—and see a job well done. All the people who wanted more than anything else to prove themselves right and the other person wrong—they could look on and be satisfied by the silence of the adversary.

But, at that moment, Nicodemus could no longer join them. Because he wasn't looking on the scene for an argument. He wasn't there to be proved right. He had seen something noble and compassionate in the way Jesus had died, the way He thought of others, the way He forgave.

Nicodemus finally looked on this Christ in terms of his own need as a human being.

Standing there at the foot of the cross, he realized that pride was just too heavy a burden to bear. Always trying to defend yourself was too wearisome a struggle. Always hiding behind the truth was too self-defeating. It was time to let the truth sink into his own heart. It was time to accept that medicine that had been offered to him months before: "You must be born again."

And so, Nicodemus took the big step. He hurried back into Jerusalem and procured a mixture of myrrh and aloes, the spices used for embalming. And he came back to the cross bearing these gifts.

Another colleague from the Sanhedrin, Joseph of Arimathea, had received permission from Pilate to bury the body of Jesus. So as the other members of the Sanhedrin watched in shock and amazement, Joseph and Nicodemus gently took His mangled body down from the cross. They had to detach it from the spikes driven into the wood. They had to wipe the blood from His face as best they could. And they wrapped Jesus in burial clothes along with the myrrh and aloes.

Then they reverently carried Him to Joseph's garden tomb. And as Nicodemus carried the noblest person he'd ever known, he was sure that pride was too heavy a burden to carry. It was much better, far better, to bear the yoke of this Christ, to accept the hard truth that pierces the heart. It was far better to stop trying to be right all the time and start out as a needy human being at the foot of the cross.

Friends, pride is just too heavy a burden to carry. Always defending ourselves is too wearisome a struggle. Why not lay all this baggage down at the foot of the cross? Why not stop hiding behind the truth? Let the truth that Christ speaks pierce your own heart.

He Saved Me From the Sidelines

The ancient Pool of Bethesda in Jerusalem was a place of despair for one man for much of his life. He lay there for a long, long time—watching the world go by, unable to be a part of it. Yet he was the same person, inside, that he'd always been. He had the same talents, the same insights. But his mind just couldn't make his body work anymore. And so he'd been condemned to the sidelines.

Worst of all, he'd fixed all his hope—every bit of the hope he could still muster—on the wrong thing!

Jerusalem was in the midst of a great festival, one that drew thousands of pilgrims from all over Israel to the city's holy temple. Among those crowding the streets and the temple court was Jesus. He had gone there to participate in the ancient rituals, like any faithful Jew.

But on this particular day, He must have been looking for a break from all the elaborate ceremonies. It was a high Sabbath, full of pomp and pageantry. And Jesus took a walk to get some fresh air.

He also wanted to get away from the priests and scribes who were always challenging Him, always trying to trap Him with trick questions. Jesus found Himself in constant conflict with the legalistic, oppressive religion of His day.

As He strolled, Jesus was soon drawn to His more natural environment—the places where the poor and afflicted huddled. This teacher from Galilee found Himself in one of the darkest corners of Jerusalem: the Pool of Bethesda.

It was dark, because it attracted human misery; it attracted people who had to hope against hope.

Jesus walked through the covered colonnades surrounding the spring-fed pool and looked around. He gazed intently at the human wreckage hovering near the water. Pale bodies wracked by fatal diseases panted on filthy mats. Their faces were turned toward the motionless surface of the pool. The blind crouched on the stone porches, their heads cocked, ready to spring toward the first sound of water lapping on stone. The maimed sprawled in a variety of positions, trying to keep their good limbs ready for action. And the most pathetic, those completely paralyzed, stared helplessly up at the cold columns.

Jesus sensed what these individuals were feeling. He sensed something of what it was like to wait there each day, day after day, and watch the sun crawl across the sky overhead. And He wanted to heal them all. Right then—right there.

But He realized that would cause a problem. To perform such a mighty miracle during this Sabbath feast day in a Jerusalem bulging with pilgrims would cut short His ministry.

Over-enthusiastic crowds had already prevented Him from ministering in certain areas. He had to be careful not to bring His conflict with the religious leaders to a head too soon.

Still, Jesus' gaze fastened on one particular case, a hopeless case, a man who'd been an invalid for 38 years. He'd been lying there, watching people come and go, for almost four decades. Once he'd been as strong and active as any other man. Once he'd been a part of the life of Jerusalem. He had worked, he may have raised a family.

But his illness had condemned him to a life on the sidelines. He wasn't a part of anything, or anyone, anymore. He just had to lie there as life passed him by.

When Jesus looked into this gray, grim face, He felt He just had to perform one miracle. He had to try to save this man from the sidelines.

Have you ever felt trapped on the sidelines? You probably haven't been paralyzed for 38 years like that man by the Pool of Bethesda. But a lot of us go through times in our lives when we do feel sidelined, when we feel life is passing us by—and we can't do anything about it.

Perhaps it's a chronic illness, something that keeps returning over and over again. You've tried all kinds of remedies, but nothing seems to work. You've been disappointed so many times. Because just when you start feeling that maybe, just maybe, you've licked this disease—it flares up again and lays you low.

Sidelined again.

Perhaps you're recovering from a divorce or the death of a loved one. You've lost something precious. And the break-up of that relationship seems to have broken up your whole world. You trudge through each day; you go through the motions. But you feel so disconnected. You're not really a part of the life around you. You don't fit in anymore.

Sidelined.

Perhaps you've lost your job. You're desperately trying to find something new, but you keep running into closed doors. Things fall through. And you watch all the other people heading off to work in the morning, all the other people busy with their routines, and you feel terribly sidelined. Life is passing you by.

This paralyzed man by the Pool of Bethesda represented the sorrow of the sidelined. He embodied all their frustration. He looked down at his limbs every day. He saw that everything was there. And yet nothing worked!

He didn't want to simply adjust to the situation. He didn't want to just cope. He wanted to get moving again!

This is the need that Jesus wanted to meet as He approached the paralytic lying on his filthy mat. But the Great Physician faced a problem. The problem was this man's faith. That's right, the problem was his faith. Why? Because he was investing it in the wrong thing. He was looking in the wrong direction.

When Jesus walked up to him and graciously asked, " 'Do you want to be made well?' " (John 5:6, NKJV), this is what the man replied: " 'Sir, I have no man to put me into the pool when the water is stirred up; but while I am coming, another steps down before me' " (John 5:7, NKJV).

This paralytic had placed his faith in the same superstition as everyone else waiting expectantly by that pool. It was said that on occasion an angel from heaven would come down to stir up the water. And whoever got into the pool first would be healed of whatever disease he or she had.

Now, it's not uncommon for spring-fed pools to bubble up sometimes, due simply to the flow of water. The so-called Fountain of the Virgin in Jerusalem exhibits the phenomenon to this day.

But the desperate people at Bethesda believed, or tried to believe, that an angel was involved—and that healing would follow.

The paralytic spent hours staring at the surface of the pool. Some other veterans of Bethesda crawled close to the water—when they smelled sheep. The Sheep Gate Market lay close by. And they imagined that a breeze strong enough to bring them the pungent odors of animals might be strong enough to help that angel disturb the pool. Others had trained themselves to detect a faint rumbling underground that was usually followed by heated water bubbling to the surface.

Tragically, they were all looking in the wrong direction. And Jesus longed to do something about it.

You know, when we're sidelined, it's very easy to look in the wrong direction. It's very easy to invest our faith in the wrong thing. We want the problem to go away—*now*. We want a magical solution.

And so we fall for job offers that are too good to be true, or miracle herbs that are too good to be true, or whirlwind romances that are too good to be true.

Recently I received a letter from a mother, Doris, who had lost two young sons—a three-year-old boy and a 16-month-old baby. Both had drowned in a backyard swimming pool.

This was a devastating tragedy, of course. How can you cope with something like that? Under the circumstances, it was very easy for Doris to simply be overwhelmed by guilt and despair. If only she'd been watching them more closely. If only she'd come a few seconds earlier. If only, if only.

This is the kind of misfortune that condemns many people to the sidelines. Their loved ones are gone. What's the point of trying anymore? What's the point of living?

So people often just bury themselves in alcohol or drugs. They find a way to escape from the pain. But they're looking for help in the wrong direction. Placing their faith in the wrong things.

Jesus had to deal with this problem. He had to deal with this man's misplaced faith.

So Jesus didn't respond to him, in the way he hoped. There was a request hidden in the paralytic's statement: " 'I have no man to put me into the pool.' "

He'd managed to persuade acquaintances to carry him to Bethesda, but no one wanted to hang around all day waiting for the water to move. Maybe, just maybe, this kind stranger would give him a push at the right time. That's all he could hope for because his faith was fixed so intently on the magical pool of water.

Christ wanted Him to look elsewhere. He wanted the paralytic to look into His face, to make a connection. So he didn't answer the man's request.

Instead, He gave him what seemed to be a perfectly ridiculous command: "Get up! Pick up your mat and walk."

Well, Jesus might as well have told the stone columns to dance in a circle around the afflicted. There was no way in the world this man could get up and walk. He'd been sidelined for 38 years.

But something happened when this startled paralytic looked intently into the face of Jesus. Who is this Man, he wondered, who can speak such words? And suddenly those muted nerve endings and shriveled limbs responded—as if they'd taken on a life of their own. The paralytic wanted to obey this impossible command. He struggled to his feet. And suddenly 38 years of immobility vanished.

He'd been saved from the sidelines.

I'd like you to think for a moment about whatever problem has condemned you to the sidelines. Think about how you react when you feel life is passing you by. Think about where you tend to place your faith.

Have you been looking in the right direction? Are you seeing the face of God in that direction? or are you obsessing over some quick fix, some magical solution that forms a detour around Him?

Sometimes we remain stuck on the sidelines because we get stuck staring at the wrong thing. And what Christ wants to do, first of all, is to get us looking into His face.

"Please," He says to all those who feel paralyzed by life, "look at Me first."

Let me tell you what happened to Doris, the woman whose two young sons drowned so tragically.

After going through a very difficult period of grief, she managed to do exactly what that paralytic did. She began looking at Jesus—intently.

She realized her life was worth living, if God could use her in some way. And that her life was in His hands. So she placed her trust in Him. And she began to experience an intense desire to get closer to God, to walk with Him each day. She found that this even made her feel closer to her two lost sons.

Listen to the words she wrote in her letter: "Now I hunger and thirst after God because of my love for Him. I know what it means to depend on Him fully; to seek Him with my whole head, to love Him from my innermost being. I know how it feels . . . when God touches your soul and comforts you. I know how it feels to rest my head on His bosom."

This woman looked intently at Jesus in her darkest hour. And she found a way out of the sidelines.

The loss of a job doesn't have to condemn you to the sidelines. Chronic illness doesn't have to condemn you to the sidelines. The loss of a loved one doesn't have to condemn you to the sidelines. There's a way out, but it starts by looking in the right direction.

Remember that Christ didn't answer the paralytic in the way he had hoped. Instead He gave him something much better.

Sometimes our fervent prayers for an immediate solution get in the way of our experiencing a bigger solution. Sometimes we keep begging God for immediate physical healing when He wants us FIRST to experience a more important emotional healing. Sometimes we keep begging God for a certain job when He wants to open up a whole new career for us. Sometimes we demand that God make so-and-so fall in love with us when He has someone much better in mind.

Focusing completely on the immediate solution can get in the way of God giving us the bigger solution. We're so fixed on the surface of the pool that we don't notice the greatest Healer of all time reaching out His hand to us.

First, look at Jesus. That's what the paralytic had to do. First, invest your faith in the right place, begin a relationship with Him. Then He can lead you out of the sidelines. He can make you part of His abundant life again. He can get you back in the race.

Listen to how Paul pictured the race of life in Hebrews 12: ". . . let us run with endurance the race that is set before us, looking unto Jesus, the author and finisher of our faith" (Hebrews 12:1, 2, NKJV).

How do we get off the sidelines and into the race? By first looking at Jesus, by first, fixing our eyes on Jesus.

Looking at Jesus creates faith. It creates trust. It creates confidence. The paralytic first had to look away from that pool of water—and into the face of the One who could really rescue him: Jesus Christ.

But there's a second thing this man had to do. There's a second thing we all must do to get off the sidelines.

The paralytic listened to Jesus. He entered into a dialogue with this stranger bending over him. He heard the question, "Do you want to be made well?" And he listened to the command, "Rise, take up your bed and walk."

After we look, we must listen. After we fix our eyes on the object of our faith, on Jesus, then we must listen to Him speak. And we must listen regularly. How? By spending time in prayer and the study of the Bible. That's how we communicate with Christ. That's how He communicates with us.

Listen to how Isaiah 50 pictures this relationship: "He awakens Me morning by morning, He awakens My ear to listen as a disciple. The Lord God has opened My ear; and I was not disobedient, nor did I turn back" (Isaiah 50:4, 5, NASB).

How do we listen as a disciple morning by morning? By listening to the Word of God. By letting Him speak His wisdom and encouragement to us through the Word.

It takes time. It takes a personal commitment. But the experience of having God speak to you is worth any investment.

How do we get off the sidelines? First, look at Jesus. Then listen to Jesus. That's what the paralytic did. And finally he did one more thing. He started to live in Jesus.

When Jesus commanded him to rise what did he do? He got up. God's power within this man enabled him to get up. When Jesus commanded him to take up his mat what did he do? He took it up. He walked away from that place of despair and sickness with the mat under his arm.

He was responding to Jesus. He was living in Jesus. That's the third thing we must do to get off the sidelines. Live in Jesus. Paul tells us in Romans: ". . . count yourselves dead to sin but alive to God in Christ Jesus" (Romans 6:11, NIV).

Dead to sin. Alive to God. The paralytic turned away completely from his old life. He wasn't going to hang around the pool of Bethesda anymore. Too many bad memories. Too many long hours of misery. He was alive to God, alive to Christ. Every fiber in his body was responding to that command to rise and walk. It was exhilarating.

We need to look at Jesus. We need to listen to Jesus. And we need to live in Jesus. We need to respond whole-heartedly to what He tells us. We need to base our lives on His teaching.

That's how we get off the sidelines. That's how we get into the race of life.

Let me tell you about a different kind of "paralyzed" man. We find him in the nineteenth century off the coast of England. One cloudy day, passengers aboard the English steamboat, Ariel, were informed that a bad storm was brewing just ahead. So they all quickly went below decks.

But one passenger approached the captain with an odd request. He wanted to be lashed to a mast on the deck. The captain stared in surprise at this very small, elderly gentleman with a weathered face. His sharp gray eyes seemed very determined. So, at length, crew members did as the man asked.

The steamboat sailed into the teeth of the storm. For four hours, the wind drove waves furiously around the boat. And the passenger stood there paralyzed, helpless. He knew he would be terribly frightened. He knew he wouldn't be able to stay above decks if given a choice.

But he wanted, as he said later, to really see the storm, to feel the storm, to have the storm blow itself into him until he became a part of it. That's why he had himself bound to a mast.

After this experience, the passenger, William Turner, went back to his studio and painted a remarkable picture that captured the awesome energy of the elements. It became one of the great artist's masterpieces.

You may feel paralyzed by forces much greater than yourself. You may feel helpless in the middle of your storm. But Jesus says, "I can save you from the sidelines. And I can do more. I can use that storm to help you create a great picture with your life. I believe there's a masterpiece in there somewhere."

Friends, look up right now. Start looking in the right direction. Look deeply into the face of Jesus. That's the first step out of the sidelines.

He Showed Me
Real Courage

It had been a long, stormy night on the Sea of Galilee. And in the morning's early light, four fishermen had beached their two fishing vessels—with nothing to show for hours of toil. They dragged several casting nets from the boats and began throwing them and pulling them through the water, to clear the nets of debris.

One of the bearded, deeply tanned men cut quite an imposing figure. His name was Peter, the leader of the group. He beckoned to some of his hired men and pointed out spots in the nets that needed mending. He was not in a good mood. Peter did not take failure lightly.

Engrossed in cleaning out the boats, he didn't notice at first, that a large crowd was starting to gather on the shore. Suddenly, he looked up and hundreds of people were standing there—and in the middle of them all, a Man he thought he recognized. The Man began to speak. Yes, it was the Teacher from Nazareth.

Peter was about to have an extraordinary encounter with Jesus, an encounter that would turn his world upside down.

For many people, it seems that religion is fine—for the weak, for those who can't get around on their own. Some people just need the comfort and reassurance of faith.

But the strong, the secure and able-bodied—well, they seem to be doing quite well on their own, thank you. Religion, for them, just seems to be something that slows you down.

But, we're going to meet a dynamic, self-sufficient individual who had to face the question—do you have to become weak to become a Christian?

That individual was Peter the fisherman. We meet him on the shore of this lake, the Sea of Galilee, after a long night of unsuccessful fishing. Jesus arrived on the scene and began teaching a crowd.

Peter listened as he worked on his boat. He had liked Jesus from the moment they met. He was so different from the scribes and priests who were always nitpicking about some detail of the law.

In fact, He was different from almost all the religious people Peter knew. He seemed to belong out here in the great outdoors. There was a sense of power in His bearing that matched the elements.

The crowd kept thickening on the beach. People in the back tried to push their way closer. And Jesus found Himself stepping back into the water. So He turned and asked Peter if He could get in his boat. The fisherman was happy to oblige.

After Jesus had finished His talk, He suggested something quite unexpected: "Let's go fishing." He asked Peter to take the boat out to deep water and let down his nets.

Peter looked at Jesus in surprise and then explained, "We worked hard all night and caught nothing." Prime fishing hours were always at night. No one caught much in broad daylight. But Peter caught the earnest look in Jesus' eyes and said, " 'but at Your bidding I will let down the nets' " (Luke 5:5, NASB).

The fisherman adjusted the sail and pointed the bow of his vessel out toward the middle of the lake. As he sat there in the stern, with the cool wind off the water blowing through his beard, he didn't realize that he was sailing out to meet his destiny.

This was to be a turning point in his life. Jesus planned to ask Peter to be His full-time disciple, to leave his fishing business and follow Him on the road. And Peter presented a special problem.

It wasn't that he couldn't make decisions. Peter usually made them instantly, let the chips fall where they may. It wasn't that Peter shrank from challenges. He thrived on them. He would butt heads with any man, take on any obstacle.

The problem was, Jesus' call consisted of two words: "Follow Me," and Peter was anything but a follower. Peter was a born leader, a confident man, a provider. He'd made good in the fishing business. He didn't need anybody to hold his hand.

Peter's temperament stands out clearly in his later contacts with Jesus. He wanted to be a player in the game. If Jesus was out walking on the water, then *he* wanted to walk on the water. If Jesus asked for a declaration of faith, then Peter would be first to give it.

Once, on a mountaintop, Jesus was transfigured before Peter and two other disciples. He appeared in awesome, divine glory, along with Moses and Elijah. What was Peter's response? It's great to be here," He said. "Let's build three temples, one for each of you."

On another occasion, when Jesus spoke of the sufferings that awaited Him, Peter took Him aside and tried to straighten Him out. " 'Far be it from You, Lord; this shall not happen to You!' " (Matthew 16:22, NKJV).

Peter embodied the strong, self-confident man. It wasn't that He didn't admire and love Jesus. He just wasn't a follower.

Weak people, needy people, followed Jesus easily, it

seemed. The lame were healed, the blind given sight, the paralyzed lifted to their feet. These individuals naturally wanted to follow the powerful, miracle-working Christ.

But what about Peter?

As he sailed out into the middle of the Sea of Galilee, he was about to face an important question: Do you have to become weak to become a follower of Christ?

Many people today face a challenge similar to Peter's. Strong, self-sufficient individuals wonder what religion has for them. They see people whose lives are falling apart collapse into God's arms. They see the hurting and the broken come for restoration. They hear calls to bring their miserable lives to Jesus, to lay their burdens down at the foot of the cross. That's fine for some. But they don't feel particularly burdened or broken. So they conclude religion isn't really for them.

Many men have this kind of reaction. They see themselves, above all, as providers. They want to take care of business. They want to be strong. And then someone comes along and makes an appeal to "Come to Jesus with all your troubles." Well, that seems passive, submissive, it seems like giving up. They can't imagine that the object of life is to have someone else take care of you.

Do you have to become weak in order to become a Christian? That's the question strong, secure people face today. And it's a question Peter faced as he sailed out on the Sea of Galilee.

How would Jesus make a disciple out of someone who was anything but a follower? Well, let's find out.

Peter let down the sail as his boat reached a deep part of the lake. Then, just as Jesus had instructed, he threw out a net. It sank into the water and, almost immediately, began to fill with fish—it seemed like a whole school of fish.

Peter couldn't believe his eyes. He and his brother Andrew started to haul in the net, but it was too heavy. The net began ripping. They had to call over to their partners in another boat to help them raise the catch. Peter filled the other boat, but the net was still bulging. They dumped fish into their own boat until it actually began to sink.

Now, Peter was really overwhelmed. He knew this lake like the palm of his hand. He knew fishing. There was no way in the world you could make a catch like this in broad daylight. There had been nothing at this spot the previous night. But here this teacher had produced the catch of the year with one little suggestion. This was an extraordinary Man, a great Man!

Impulsive Peter threw himself down at Jesus' feet and said the first thing that popped into his head, "Depart from me, for I am a sinful man, O Lord!"

And Jesus changed his life with one sentence, "From now on you will catch men." That was the call. That was the appeal. How did Jesus make a disciple out of someone who was anything but a follower? He showed him how much *more* he could do—joined to Himself. He fired his imagination. He opened up possibilities. Two boatloads of fish did that. That's why Peter responded when Christ said, "Follow Me and I will make you a fisher of men."

Luke tells us that after he brought his fishing vessels to the shore, Peter left everything and followed Jesus.

Christ has a special message for the strong: Follow Me, and you can do more than you ever dreamed possible. You can do more, not less.

Listen to the benediction that Paul, another very strong individual, wrote in his letter to the Ephesians: "Now to him who is able to do immeasurably more than all we ask or imagine, according to his power that is at work within us, to him be glory" (Ephesians 3:20, NIV).

Two boats filled with fish were immeasurably more than Peter could have imagined. He was overwhelmed by the power and nobility of Christ. And so he set out on the road with Him.

But that was just the beginning of the story. That was just the beginning of a series of adventures that were to change Peter's life. This strong, self-sufficient individual had been attracted to Christ because of a big challenge—becoming a fisher of men. But now he had a very important lesson to learn, and it would take him a long time to learn it.

Peter had to become strong in a different way. He had to become bold and courageous in a different way. It wasn't enough to simply join forces with Christ. The power of Christ had to get inside him some way.

That power, that spiritual strength, did get into Peter's heart and soul. Christ did transform him—although we don't see it clearly until after Jesus goes back up to heaven. Let me give you a few examples of that transformation, that different kind of strength.

Strong, secure people tend to say whatever's on their minds, without fretting about the consequences. Peter was certainly that way. But he was also very impulsive and tended to get his foot caught in his mouth a lot. We see that throughout the gospels.

But take a look at him later, in the book of Acts. Once he was brought before a Jewish council for speaking about Jesus at the temple. He had just been imprisoned for doing that and now he was at it again.

The Jewish officials put on their most indignant faces. "You have filled Jerusalem with your doctrine," they thundered.

The officials were sure they could intimidate this former fisherman who stood before them. After all, this was Peter, who, when Jesus was arrested, had run away with the other disciples. At Jesus' trial, he had denied to a servant that he even knew Jesus. They just needed to get

Peter's impulses going in the right direction.

But instead of apologizing and promising not to speak again, Peter replied calmly, "We ought to obey God rather than men." And he went on to remind them that they had condemned Jesus to death on a cross, and that God had raised Him from the dead and exalted Him to heaven. Peter ended with his assertion, " 'We are His witnesses to these things' " (Acts 5:32, NKJV).

The Jewish officials didn't quite know what to do. This was a different man standing before them. This was a different kind of strength, a steadier resolve.

In the end, they gave Peter and his companions another warning, had them beaten, and sent them on their way. Peter rejoiced that He could suffer shame in Christ's name.

Yes, something had happened to that fisherman. Before, when Peter spoke, he had to take his foot out of his mouth. Now, when Peter spoke, thousands were converted.

Peter had displayed a certain kind of courage before. When Jesus warned that His disciples would forsake Him in the hour of trial, Peter answered back: . . . " 'Even if all fall away on account of you, I never will.' " . . . " 'Even if I have to die with you, I will never disown you' " (Matthew 26:33, 35, NIV).

And Peter meant those words. He *was* willing to die like a man for the cause of Christ.

He was also willing to fight like a man. When soldiers arrived in the Garden of Gethsemane, Peter drew his sword. As they stepped forward to arrest Jesus, he lunged forward and cut off the ear of the high priest's servant. Jesus had to tell him to put his weapon away.

But then, when Jesus allowed Himself to be dragged away, Peter's resolve vanished. He found himself running for his life, in the night, along with the other disciples.

Peter was prepared to fight for Jesus. But he wasn't

prepared to be mocked because of Jesus. That same night, a servant girl thought she recognized Peter and taunted him as one of Jesus' Galilean followers. Others joined in. Peter swore angrily, "I don't know the man!" Before he knew it, he'd denied the One who meant everything to him.

Peter thought he would be the one to stand strong in the worst of times. But he buckled under pressure like everyone else.

Later, however, in the book of Acts, we find this same man showing us a very different kind of courage. He was in prison again for preaching openly in the name of Christ. King Herod had arrested him this time. He intended to have Peter executed to score points with some of his Jewish subjects.

But in the middle of the night, an angel came to rescue Peter. He appeared in the cell where the apostle was chained between two soldiers. He was going to lead him out to safety. The chains would fall off and the prison doors would open.

But here's a remarkable detail that stands out in the narrative. The book of Acts tells us that the angel had to wake Peter up! He had to strike him on the side and say, "Quick, get up!"

Think about that. Here's a man who is going to come up for trial the next day. And the trial is fixed. He's probably going to be condemned to death. Any normal person would be pacing in that cell, worrying, fretting, sweating it out. But Peter was sound asleep.

Peter made courageous stands for Christ throughout the book of Acts. But this one detail speaks volumes about the kind of courage that had entered his heart. It contrasts with the bravado of a man who swears allegiance to Christ one minute and denies knowing him the next.

In that dungeon cell, Peter had a calm assurance that

he was in God's hands. He was doing God's work; God was responsible for the ultimate outcome.

To put it in a nutshell. Peter was no longer trying to be brave on his own. He was no longer trying to *look* courageous. He just was.

So, we've seen these contrasts between Peter before and Peter after. We've seen the difference between a man who thought he was strong and a man who really did find inner strength.

What made the difference? What happened to Peter?

To understand, let's look at his failure. After he denied Christ, Peter had to take a good, hard look at himself. Peter was a doer, a mover, a shaker, a very self-confident man. He wasn't used to taking good, hard looks at himself. But now, he had to face his weaknesses, his vulnerability.

And this finally enabled him to open up to the kind of strength that Christ has to offer. It enabled him to accept his need of a deeper kind of courage. The love of Christ broke through. It won him over. And so when the Holy Spirit was poured out on the Day of Pentecost, Peter received it wholeheartedly. He was ready. Pride no longer put up barriers. He wasn't posturing as the self-sufficient one; he was pleading as the one in need.

We get a glimpse of what Peter learned in his first letter. Listen to what he wrote: "Each one should use whatever gift he has received to serve others, faithfully administering God's grace in its various forms. If anyone speaks, he should do it as one speaking the very words of God. If anyone serves, he should do it with the strength God provides, so that in all things God may be praised through Jesus Christ" (1 Peter 4:10,11, NIV).

This admonition is really a picture of Peter's new life. He wasn't just trying hard on his own. He was aware of God's gift, of God's grace, working inside him. When he spoke, it wasn't just his own eloquence that counted, it was God's words expressed through Him. When he served, he served with the strength that God provided.

Did Peter become a weak person after his conversion? Not at all. He found a more resilient strength. He found a deeper courage.

But did this strong person have to come to understand his weakness? Yes. He had to see that he couldn't do it on his own. He had to see that, to stand strong you have to stand with Christ.

Before, Peter's courage was a little like tin armor, a bit brittle, with a hollow echo inside. After, Peter's courage was like tempered steel.

Do you have to become weak to become a Christian? No. But you have to acknowledge your weakness in order to become truly strong.

The most powerful personality in history invites you to share in His life. He wants to pour a more resilient strength inside you, a deeper courage inside you. The most powerful and most loving personality in history wants to change you from the inside out.

But you have to come to Him acknowledging your need, without posturing, without pretensions. You have to come just as you are. Let's join Peter right now as we respond to Christ's great call, "Follow Me."